quick and simple recipes
desserts

Contents

Culinary Terms Explained

BAIN MARIE A shallow tin, often a roasting tin, half-filled with water. Smaller dishes of food are then placed in it, allowing them to cook at lower temperatures without over-heating.

BAKING BLIND The method often used for cooking the pastry case of flans and tarts before the filling is added.

BAKING POWDER A raising agent which works by producing carbon dioxide bubbles which expand during the baking process and make the breads and cakes rise.

BEATING The method by which air is introduced into a mixture using a fork, wooden spoon, whisk or electric mixer. Beating is also used as a method to soften ingredients.

BICARBONATE OF SODA This acts as a raising agent in baking when combined with liquid.

BINDING Adding liquid or egg to bring a dry mixture together.

BLENDER An electric machine with rotating blades used mainly with soft and wet ingredients to purée and liquidise, although it can grind dry ingredients such as nuts and breadcrumbs.

CENTIGRADE This is a scale for measuring the temperature within the oven (also known as celsius).

CHOUX A type of pastry (rather like a glossy batter) that is piped into small balls on to a baking tray and baked until light and airy. They can then be filled with cream or savoury fillings.

COCOTTE See Ramekin

CORNSTARCH/CORNFLOUR A dense flour, which is used as a thickening agent.

CREAM OF TARTAR Another raising agent often present in both self-raising flour and baking powder.

CREAMING The method by which fat and sugar are beaten together until lighter in colour and fluffy. By creaming the fat in cake mixtures, air is incorporated into the fat, lightening the texture.

CRIMPING The fluted effect used for the decoration on pies or tarts created by pinching the edge crust.

CRUMB The term by which flour and fat are combined typically for use in pastry, crumble and biscuits.

CURDLE When the milk separates from a sauce through acidity or excessive heat. This can also happen to creamed cake mixtures that have separated due to the eggs being too cold or added too quickly.

DOUGH A dense mixture of flour, water and, often yeast. Also used to describe raw pastry, scones and biscuit mixtures.

DREDGING The sprinkling of food with a coating (generally of flour or sugar).

DROPPING CONSISTENCY The consistency that a cake or pudding mixture should reach before being cooked. It tends to be fairly soft (but not runny) and should drop off a spoon in around five seconds when tapped lightly on the side of a bowl.

DUST To sprinkle lightly, often with flour, sugar or icing sugar.

EN CROÛTE Used to describe food which is covered with raw pastry and then baked.

FILO A type of pastry that is wafer-thin. Three to four sheets are usually used at a time in baking.

FOLDING A method of combining creamed fat and sugar with flour in cake and pudding mixes usually by carefully mixing with a large metal spoon, in order to maintain a light texture.

GLACÉ A French term meaning glossy or iced. Glacé icing is a quick icing often used to decorate cakes and biscuits. It is made using icing sugar and warm water.

GREASEPROOF PAPER Paper that tends to be relatively non-stick and which is used to line tins to prevent cakes and puddings from sticking.

KNEAD The process of pummelling and working dough in order to strengthen the gluten in the flour and make the dough more elastic, thus giving a good rise.

KNOCK BACK The term used for a second kneading after the dough has been allowed to rise. This is done to disperse any large pockets of air.

PASTEURISATION A treatment to destroy the bacteria found in fermentable liquides, such as milk, and enable it to be kept for longer. It is also applied to prepackaged food and eggs.

PUFF PASTRY Multilayered pastry, made by placing butter between layers of dough which is then repeatedly rolled out. The butter creates steam during baking, which causes the pastry to puff up.

RAMEKIN An ovenproof, earthenware dish which provides an individual serving.

RICE PAPER Edible paper is made from the pith of a Chinese tree and can be used as a base on which to bake sticky cakes and biscuits.

RUBBING IN The method of combining fat into flour for crumble toppings, shortcrust pastry, biscuits and scones.

SIFTING The shaking of dry ingredients (primarily flour) through a metal or nylon sieve to remove impurities and introduces air, before using in baking.

WHIPPING/WHISKING The term given to incorporating air rapidly into a mixture (either through using a manual whisk or an electric whisk).

ZEST Very thin, long pieces of the coloured part of an orange, lemon or lime peel.

Apple & Cinnamon Brown Betty

Ingredients
Serves 4

450 g/1 lb cooking
   apples
50 g/2 oz caster sugar
finely grated rind of 1
   lemon
125 g/4 oz fresh white
   breadcrumbs
125 g/4 oz demerara
   sugar
½ tsp ground cinnamon
25 g/1 oz butter

For the custard

3 medium egg yolks
1 tbsp caster sugar
500 ml/1 pint milk
1 tbsp cornflour
few drops of vanilla
   essence

1 Preheat the oven to 180°C/ 350°F/Gas Mark 4. Lightly oil a 900 ml/1½ pint ovenproof dish. Peel, core and slice the apples and place in a saucepan with the caster sugar, lemon rind and 2 tablespoons of water. Simmer for 10–15 minutes or until tender.

2 Mix the breadcrumbs with the sugar and the cinnamon. Place half the sweetened apples in the base of the prepared dish and spoon over half of the crumb mixture. Place the remaining apples on top and cover with the rest of the crumb mixture.

3 Melt the butter and pour over the surface of the pudding. Cover the dish with non-stick baking paper and bake in the preheated oven for 20 minutes. Remove the paper and bake for a further 10–15 minutes, or until golden.

4 Meanwhile, make the custard by whisking the egg yolks and sugar together until creamy. Mix 1 tablespoon of the milk with the cornflour, until a paste forms and reserve.

5 Warm the rest of the milk until nearly boiling and pour over the egg mixture with the paste and vanilla essence.

6 Place the bowl over a sauce pan of gently simmering water. Stir over the heat until thickened and can coat the back of a spoon. Strain into a jug and serve hot over the pudding.

Baked Lemon & Sultana Cheesecake

Ingredients
Cuts into 10 slices

275 g/10 oz caster sugar
50 g/2 oz butter
50 g/2 oz self-raising
   flour
½ level tsp baking
   powder
5 large eggs
450 g/1 lb cream cheese
40 g/1½ oz plain flour
grated rind of 1 lemon
3 tbsp fresh lemon
   juice
150 ml/¼ pint crème
   fraîche
75 g/3 oz sultanas

To decorate

1 tbsp icing sugar
fresh blackcurrants or
   blueberries
mint leaves

1 Preheat the oven to 170°C/ 325°F/Gas Mark 3. Oil a 20.5 cm/8 inch loose-bottomed round cake tin with non-stick baking paper.

2 Beat 50 g/2 oz of the sugar and the butter together until light and creamy, then stir in the self-raising flour, baking powder and 1 egg.

3 Mix lightly together until well blended. Spoon into the prepared tin and spread the mixture over the base. Separate the 4 remaining eggs and reserve.

4 Blend the cheese in a food processor until soft. Gradually add the eggs yolks and sugar and blend until smooth. Turn into a bowl and stir in the rest of the flour, lemon rind and juice.

5 Mix lightly before adding the crème fraîche and sultanas, stirring well.

6 Whisk the egg whites until stiff, fold into the cheese mixture and pour into the tin. Tap lightly on the surface to remove any air bubbles. Bake in the preheated oven for about 1 hour, or until golden and firm.

7 Cover lightly if browning too much. Switch the oven off and leave in the oven to cool for 2–3 hours.

8 Remove the cheesecake from the oven and when completely cold remove from the tin. Sprinkle with the icing sugar, decorate with the blackcurrants or blueberries and mint leaves and serve.

Cherry Batter Pudding

Ingredients
Serves 4

450 g/1 lb fresh cherries
(or 425 g can
pitted cherries)
50 g/2 oz plain flour
pinch of salt
3 tbsp caster sugar
2 medium eggs
300 ml/½ pint milk
40 g/1½ oz butter
1 tbsp rum
extra caster sugar, to
dredge
fresh cream, to serve

1 Preheat the oven to 220°C/ 425°F/Gas Mark 7. Lightly oil a 900 ml/1½ pint shallow baking dish.

2 Rinse the cherries, drain well and remove the stones (using a cherry stoner if possible). If using canned cherries, drain well, discard the juice and place in the prepared dish.

3 Sift the flour and salt into a large bowl. Stir in 2 tablespoons of the caster sugar and make a well in the centre. Beat the eggs, then pour into the well of the dry ingredients.

4 Warm the milk and slowly pour into the well, beating throughout and gradually drawing in the flour from the sides of the bowl. Continue until a smooth batter has formed.

5 Melt the butter in a small saucepan over a low heat, then stir into the batter with the rum. Reserve for 15 minutes, then beat again until smooth and easy to pour.

6 Pour into the prepared baking dish and bake in the preheated oven for 30–35 minutes, or until golden brown and set.

7 Remove the pudding from the oven, sprinkle with the remaining sugar and serve hot with plenty of fresh cream.

CHEF'S TIP
For that extra hint of cherry flavour why not replace the rum with kirsch – an eau-de-vie rather than a liqueur which is made from pine kernels and cherry fruit juice to produce a brandy.

Chocolate & Almond Daquoise with Summer Berries

Ingredients
Cuts into 8 servings

Almond meringues

6 large egg whites
$\frac{1}{4}$ tsp cream of tartar
275 g/10 oz caster sugar
$\frac{1}{2}$ tsp almond essence
50 g/2 oz blanched or
  flaked almonds, lightly
  toasted and finely
  ground

Chocolate buttercream

75 g/3 oz butter,
  softened
450 g/1 lb icing sugar,
  sifted
50 g/2 oz cocoa
  powder, sifted
3–4 tbsp milk or single
  cream
550 g/1$\frac{1}{4}$ lb mixed
  summer berries such
  as raspberries,
  strawberries and
  blackberries

To decorate

toasted flaked almonds
icing sugar

1 Preheat the oven to 140˚C/ 275˚F/Gas Mark 1,10 minutes before baking. Line three baking sheets with non-stick baking paper and draw a 20.5 cm/8 inch round on each one.

2 Whisk the egg whites and cream of tartar until soft peaks form. Gradually beat in the sugar, 2 tablespoons at a time, beating well after each addition, until the whites are stiff and glossy. Beat in the almond essence, then using a metal spoon or rubber spatula gently fold in the ground almonds. Divide the mixture evenly between the three circles of baking paper, spreading neatly into the rounds and smoothing the tops evenly.

3 Bake in the preheated oven for about 1$\frac{1}{4}$ hours or until crisp, rotating the baking sheets halfway through cooking. Turn off the oven, allow to cool for about 1 hour, then remove and cool completely before discarding the lining paper.

4 Beat the butter, icing sugar and cocoa powder until smooth and creamy, adding the milk or cream to form a soft consistency.

5 Reserve about a quarter of the berries to decorate. Spread one meringue with a third of the buttercream and top with a third of the remaining berries. Repeat until the stack is three layers high. Scatter with the toasted flaked almonds, the reserved berries and sprinkle with icing sugar to serve.

Chocolate & Saffron Cheesecake

Ingredients
Serves 6

¼ tsp saffron threads
175 g/6 oz plain flour
pinch of salt
75 g/3 oz butter, cut
  into small dice
1 tbsp caster sugar
1 medium egg yolk
350 g/12 oz curd cheese
75 g/3 oz golden
  granulated sugar
125 g/4 oz plain dark
  chocolate, melted
  and cooled
6 tbsp milk
3 medium eggs
1 tbsp icing sugar,
  sifted, to decorate

1 Preheat the oven to 200°C/ 400°F/Gas Mark 6. Lightly oil a 20.5 cm/8 inch, fluted flan tin. Soak the saffron threads in one tablespoon of hot water for 20 minutes. Sift the flour and salt into a bowl. Add the butter to the flour and using your fingertips, rub it in, until the mixture resembles breadcrumbs. Stir in the sugar.

2 Beat the egg yolk with 1 tablespoon of cold water, then add to the breadcrumb mixture to form a smooth dough. Add a little extra water if necessary. Knead on a lightly floured surface until free from cracks. Wrap in clingfilm and chill in the refrigerator for 30 minutes.

3 Roll the pastry out on a lightly floured surface and use to line the flan tin. Prick the pastry base and sides with a fork and line with nonstick baking parchment and baking beans. Bake blind in the preheated oven for 12 minutes. Remove the beans and baking parchment and continue to bake blind for 5 minutes.

4 Beat together the curd cheese and granulated sugar, then beat in the melted chocolate, saffron liquid, milk and eggs, thoroughly. Pour the mixture into the cooked flan case and place on a baking sheet. Reduce the oven temperature to 190°C/375°F/Gas Mark 5 and bake for 15 minutes, then reduce the oven temperature to 180°C/ 350°F/Gas Mark 4 and continue to bake for 20–30 minutes, or until set.

6 Remove from the oven and leave for 10 minutes before removing from the flan tin, if serving warm. If serving cold, leave in the flan tin to cool before removing.

Chocolate Creams

Ingredients
Serves 4

125 g/4 oz plain dark
 chocolate
1 tbsp brandy
4 medium eggs,
 separated
200 ml/7 fl oz pint
 double cream
1 tbsp caster sugar
grated rind of 1 orange
2 tbsp Cointreau
25 g/1 oz white
 chocolate
8 physalis, to decorate

1 Break the chocolate into small pieces, then place in a heatproof bowl set over a saucepan of gently simmering water. Add the brandy and heat gently, stirring occasionally until the chocolate has melted and is smooth. Remove from the heat and leave to cool slightly, then beat in the egg yolks, one at a time, beating well after each addition. Reserve.

2 Whisk the egg whites until stiff but not dry, then stir 1 tablespoon into the chocolate mixture. Add the remainder and stir in gently. Chill in the refrigerator while preparing the cream.

3 Whip the cream until just beginning to thicken, then stir in the sugar, orange rind and Cointreau and continue to whisk together until soft peaks form. Spoon the chocolate mousse into the cream mixture and using a metal spoon, fold the two mixtures together to create a marbled effect. Alternatively, continue folding the two mixtures together until mixed thoroughly. Spoon into four individual glass dishes, cover each dessert with clingfilm and chill in the refrigerator for 2 hours.

4 Using a potato peeler, shave the white chocolate into curls. Uncover the desserts and scatter over the shavings. Peel the husks back from the physalis berries and pinch together for decoration. Top each dessert with two berries and chill in the refrigerator until ready to serve.

Chocolate Fruit Tiramisu

Ingredients
Serves 4

2 ripe passion fruit
2 fresh nectarines or peaches
75 g/3 oz sponge finger biscuits
125 g/4 oz Amaretto biscuits
5 tbsp amaretti liqueur
6 tbsp prepared black coffee
250 g/9 oz mascarpone cheese
450 ml/¾ pint fresh custard
200 g/7 oz plain dark chocolate, finely chopped or grated
2 tbsp cocoa powder, sifted

1 Cut the passion fruit and scoop out the seeds and reserve. Plunge the nectarines or peaches into boiling water and leave for 2–3 minutes. Carefully remove the nectarines from the water, and remove the stones. Peel off the skin and chop the flesh finely.

2 Break the sponge finger biscuits and amaretti biscuits in half. Place the Amaretto liqueur and black coffee into a shallow dish and stir well. Place half the sponge fingers and amaretti biscuits into this mixture and soak for 30 seconds. Remove from the liquor and arrange in the bases of four deep individual glass dishes.

3 Cream the mascarpone cheese until soft and creamy, then slowly beat in the fresh custard. Spoon half the mascarpone mixture over the biscuits in the dishes and sprinkle with 125 g/4 oz of the finely chopped or grated dark chocolate.

4 Arrange half the passion fruit seeds and the chopped nectarine or peaches over the chocolate and sprinkle with half the sifted cocoa powder.

5 Place the remaining biscuits into the coffee liqueur mixture and soak for 30 seconds, then arrange on top of the fruit and cocoa powder. Top with the remaining chopped or grated chocolate, nectarine or peach and the mascarpone cheese mixture.

6 Chill in the refrigerator for 1½ hours, then spoon the remaining passion fruit seeds and cocoa powder over the desserts. Chill in the refrigerator for 30 minutes and serve.

Chocolate Mousse Cake

Ingredients
Cuts into 8–10 servings

For the cake
450 g/1 lb plain dark chocolate, chopped
125 g/4 oz butter, softened
3 tbsp brandy
9 large eggs, separated
150 g/5 oz caster sugar

Chocolate glaze
225 ml/8 fl oz double cream
225 g/8 oz plain dark chocolate, chopped
2 tbsp brandy

1 Preheat the oven to 180°C/ 350°F/Gas Mark 4 10 minutes before baking. Lightly oil and line the bases of 2 x 20.5 cm/8 inch spring-form tins with baking paper. Melt the chocolate and butter in a bowl set over a saucepan of simmering water. Stir until smooth. Remove from the heat and stir in the brandy.

2 Whisk the egg yolks and the sugar, reserving 2 tablespoons of the sugar, until thick and creamy. Slowly beat in the chocolate mixture until smooth and well blended. Whisk the egg whites until soft peaks form, then sprinkle over the remaining sugar and continue whisking until stiff but not dry.

3 Fold a large spoonful of the egg whites into the chocolate mixture. Gently fold in the remaining egg whites. Divide about two-thirds of the mixture evenly between the tins. Bake in the preheated oven for about 20 minutes, or until the cakes are well risen and set. Remove and cool for at least 1 hour.

4 Loosen the edges of the cake layers with a knife. Using the fingertips, lightly press the crusty edges down. Pour the remaining third of the mousse over one layer, spreading until even. Remove the other cake from the tin and gently invert on to the mousse, bottom side up to make a flat top layer. Discard the lining paper and chill for 4–6 hours, or until set.

5 To make the glaze, melt the cream and chocolate with the brandy in a heavy-based saucepan and stir until smooth. Cool until thickened. Unclip the side of the mousse cake and place on a wire rack. Pour over half the glaze and spread to cover. Allow to set. To serve, heat the remaining glaze and pour round each slice.

Chocolate Profiteroles

Ingredients
Serves 4

For the pastry
150 ml/¼ pint water
50 g/2 oz butter
65 g/2½ oz plain flour, sifted
2 medium eggs, lightly beaten

For the custard
300 ml/½ pint milk
pinch of freshly grated nutmeg
3 medium egg yolks
50 g/2 oz caster sugar
2 tbsp plain flour, sifted
2 tbsp cornflour, sifted

For the sauce
175 g/6 oz soft brown sugar
150 ml/¼ pint boiling water
1 tsp instant coffee
1 tbsp cocoa powder
1 tbsp brandy
75 g/3 oz butter
1 tbsp golden syrup

1 Preheat the oven to 220°C/ 425°F/Gas Mark 7, 15 minutes before cooking. Lightly oil two baking sheets. For the pastry, place the water and the butter in a heavy-based saucepan and bring to the boil. Remove from the heat and beat in the flour. Return to the heat and cook for 1 minute or until the mixture forms a ball in the centre of the saucepan.

2 Remove from the heat and leave to cool slightly, then gradually beat in the eggs a little at a time, beating well after each addition. Once all the eggs have been added, beat until the paste is smooth and glossy. Pipe or spoon 20 small balls onto the baking sheets, allowing plenty of room for expansion.

3 Bake in the preheated oven for 25 minutes or until well risen and golden brown. Reduce the oven temperature to 180°C/ 350°F/Gas Mark 4. Make a hole in each ball and continue to bake for a further 5 minutes. Remove from the oven and leave to cool.

4 For the custard, place the milk and nutmeg in a heavy-based saucepan and bring to the boil. In another saucepan, whisk together the egg yolks, sugar and the flours, then beat in the hot milk. Bring to the boil and simmer, whisking constantly for 2 minutes. Cover and leave to cool.

5 Spoon the custard into the profiteroles and arrange on a large serving dish. Place all the sauce ingredients in a small saucepan and bring to the boil, then simmer for 10 minutes. Remove from the heat and cool slightly before serving with the chocolate profiteroles.

Chocolate Sponge Pudding with Fudge Sauce

Ingredients
Serves 4

75 g/3 oz butter
75 g/3 oz caster sugar
50 g/2 oz plain dark
   chocolate, melted
50 g/2 oz self-raising
   flour
25 g/1 oz drinking
   chocolate
1 large egg
1 tbsp icing sugar, to
   dust
crème fraîche, to serve

Fudge sauce

50 g/2 oz soft light
   brown sugar
1 tbsp cocoa powder
40 g/1½ oz pecan nuts,
   roughly chopped
25 g/1 oz caster sugar
300 ml/½ pint hot,
   strong black coffee

1 Preheat the oven to 170°C/ 325°F/Gas Mark 3. Oil a 900 ml/1½ pint pie dish.

2 Cream the butter and the sugar together in a large bowl until light and fluffy. Stir in the melted chocolate, flour, drinking chocolate and egg and mix together.

3 Turn the mixture into the prepared dish and level the surface.

4 To make the fudge sauce, blend the brown sugar, cocoa powder and pecan nuts together and sprinkle evenly over the top of the pudding.

5 Stir the caster sugar into the hot black coffee until it has dissolved. Carefully pour the coffee over the top of the pudding.

6 Bake in the preheated oven for 50–60 minutes, until the top is firm to touch. There will now be a rich sauce underneath the sponge.

7 Remove from the oven, dust with icing sugar and serve hot with crème fraîche.

Creamy Puddings with Mixed Berry Compote

Ingredients
Serves 6

300 ml/½ pint half-fat double cream

1 x 250 g carton ricotta cheese

50 g/2 oz caster sugar

125 g/4 oz white chocolate, broken into pieces

350 g/12 oz mixed summer fruits such as strawberries, blueberries and raspberries

2 tbsp Cointreau

1 Set the freezer to rapid freeze. Whip the cream until soft peaks form. Fold in the ricotta cheese and half the sugar.

2 Place the chocolate in a bowl set over a saucepan of simmering water. Stir until melted.

3 Remove from the heat and leave to cool, stirring occasionally. Stir into the cheese mixture until well blended.

4 Spoon the mixture into six individual pudding moulds and level the surface of each pudding with the back of a spoon. Place in the freezer and freeze for 4 hours.

5 Place the fruits and the remaining sugar in a pan and heat gently, stirring occasionally until the sugar has dissolved and the juices are just beginning to run. Stir in the Cointreau to taste.

6 Dip the pudding moulds in hot water for 30 seconds and invert on to six serving plates. Spoon the fruit compote over the puddings and serve immediately. Remember to return the freezer to its normal setting.

Crème Brûlée with Sugared Raspberries

Ingredients
Serves 6

600 ml/1 pint fresh whipping cream
4 medium egg yolks
75 g/3 oz caster sugar
½ tsp vanilla essence
25 g/1 oz demerara sugar
175 g/6 oz fresh raspberries

1 Preheat the oven to 150°C/ 300°F/Gas Mark 2. Pour the cream into a bowl and place over a saucepan of gently simmering water. Heat gently but do not allow to boil.

2 Meanwhile, whisk together the egg yolks, 50 g/2 oz of the caster sugar and the vanilla essence. When the cream is warm, pour it over the egg mixture briskly whisking until it is mixed completely.

3 Pour into 6 individual ramekin dishes and place in a roasting tin. Fill the tin with sufficient water to come halfway up the sides of the dishes.

4 Bake in the preheated oven for about 1 hour, or until the puddings are set. (To test if set, carefully insert a round bladed knife into the centre, if the knife comes out clean they are set.)

5 Remove the puddings from the roasting tin and allow to cool. Chill in the refrigerator, preferably overnight.

6 Sprinkle the sugar over the top of each dish and place the puddings under a preheated hot grill.

7 When the sugar has caramelised and turned deep brown, remove from the heat and cool. Chill the puddings in the refrigerator for 2–3 hours before serving.

8 Toss the raspberries in the remaining caster sugar and sprinkle over the top of each dish. Serve with a little extra cream if liked.

French Chocolate Pecan Torte

Ingredients
Cuts into 16 slices

200 g/7 oz plain dark
   chocolate, chopped
150 g/5 oz butter, diced
4 large eggs
100 g/3½ oz caster
   sugar
2 tsp vanilla essence
125 g/4 oz pecans, finely
   ground
2 tsp ground cinnamon
24 pecan halves, lightly
   toasted, to decorate

Chocolate glaze

125 g/4 oz plain dark
   chocolate, chopped
60 g/2½ oz butter, diced
2 tbsp clear honey
¼ tsp ground cinnamon

1 Preheat the oven to 180°C/ 350°F/Gas Mark 4, 10 minutes before baking. Lightly butter and line a 20.5 x 5 cm/8 x 2 inch springform tin with non-stick baking paper. Wrap the tin in a large sheet of tinfoil to prevent water seeping in.

2 Melt the chocolate and butter in a saucepan over a low heat and stir until smooth. Remove from the heat and cool.

3 Using an electric whisk, beat the eggs, sugar and vanilla essence until light and foamy. Gradually beat in the melted chocolate, ground nuts and cinnamon, then pour into the prepared tin.

4 Set the foil-wrapped tin in a large roasting tin and pour in enough boiling water to come 2 cm/¾ inches up the sides of the tin. Bake in the preheated oven until the edge is set, but the centre is still soft when the tin is gently shaken. Remove from the oven and place on a wire rack to cool.

5 For the glaze, melt all the ingredients over a low heat until melted and smooth, then remove from the heat. Dip each pecan halfway into the glaze and set on a sheet of non-stick baking paper until set. Allow the remaining glaze to thicken slightly.

6 Remove the cake from the tin and invert. Pour the glaze over the cake smoothing the top and spreading the glaze around the sides. Arrange the glazed pecans around the edge of the torte. Allow to set and serve.

Iced Bakewell Tart

Ingredients
Cuts into 8 slices

For the rich pastry

175 g/6 oz plain flour
pinch of salt
60 g/2½ oz butter, cut
  into small pieces
50 g/2 oz white
  vegetable fat, cut into
  small pieces
2 small egg yolks,
  beaten

For the filling

125 g/4 oz butter, melted
125 g/4 oz caster sugar
125 g/4 oz ground
  almonds
2 large eggs, beaten
few drops of almond
  essence
2 tbsp seedless
  raspberry jam

For the icing

125 g/4 oz icing sugar,
  sifted
6–8 tsp fresh lemon
  juice
25 g/1 oz toasted flaked
  almonds

1 Preheat the oven to 200°C/ 400°F/Gas Mark 6. Place the flour and salt in a bowl, rub in the butter and vegetable fat until the mixture resembles breadcrumbs. Alternatively, blend quickly, in short bursts in a food processor.

2 Add the eggs with sufficient water to make a soft, pliable dough. Knead lightly on a floured board then chill in the refrigerator for about 30 minutes. Roll out the pastry and use to line a 23 cm/ 9 inch loose-bottomed flan tin.

3 For the filling, mix together the melted butter, sugar, almonds and beaten eggs and add a few drops of almond essence. Spread the base of the pastry case with the raspberry jam and spoon over the egg mixture.

4 Bake in the preheated oven for about 30 minutes, or until the filling is firm and golden brown. Remove from the oven and allow to cool completely.

5 When the tart is cold make the icing by mixing together the icing sugar and lemon juice, a little at a time, until the icing is smooth and of a spreadable consistency.

6 Spread the icing over the tart, leave to set for 2–3 minutes and sprinkle with the almonds. Chill in the refrigerator for about 10 minutes and serve.

Lemon & Apricot Pudding

Ingredients
Serves 4

125 g/4 oz ready-to-eat
   dried apricots
3 tbsp orange juice,
   warmed
50 g/2 oz butter
125 g/4 oz caster sugar
juice and grated rind of
   2 lemons
2 medium eggs
50 g/2 oz self-raising
   flour
300 ml/½ pint milk
custard or fresh cream,
   to serve

1 Preheat the oven to 180°C/ 350°F/Gas Mark 4. Oil a 1.1 litre/2 pint pie dish.

2 Soak the apricots in the orange juice for 10–15 minutes or until most of the juice has been absorbed, then place in the base of the pie dish.

3 Cream the butter and sugar together with the lemon rind until light and fluffy.

4 Separate the eggs. Beat the egg yolks into the creamed mixture with a spoonful of flour after each addition. Add the remaining flour and beat well until smooth.

5 Stir the milk and lemon juice into the creamed mixture. Whisk the egg whites in a grease-free mixing bowl until stiff and standing in peaks. Fold into the mixture using a metal spoon or rubber spatula.

6 Pour into the prepared dish and place in a baking tray filled with enough cold water to come halfway up the sides of the dish.

7 Bake in the preheated oven for about 45 minutes, or until the sponge is firm and golden brown. Remove from the oven. Serve immediately with the custard or fresh cream.

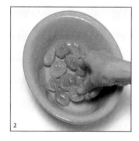

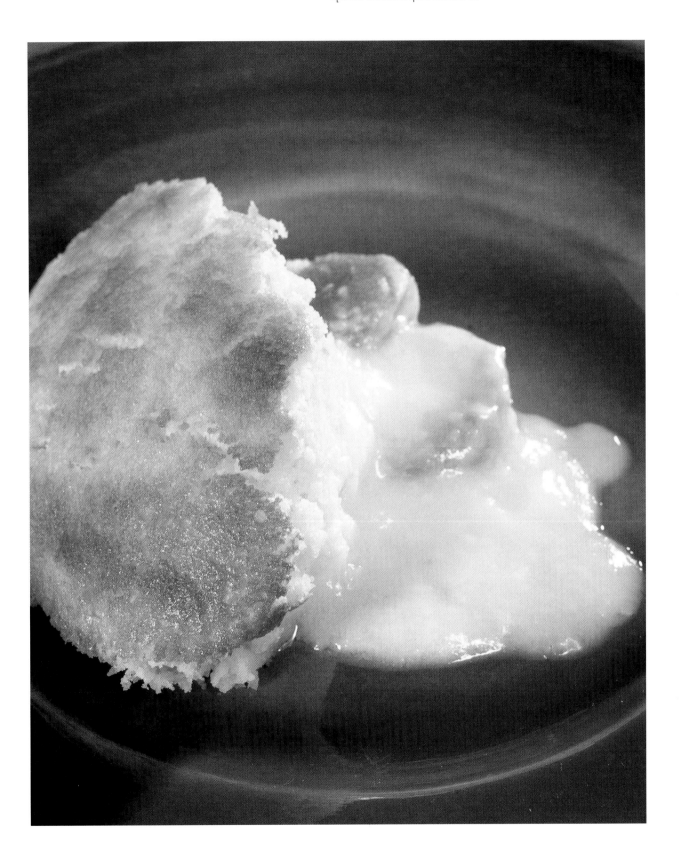

Poached Pears with Chocolate Sauce

Ingredients
Serves 4

300 ml/½ pint red wine
125 g/4 oz caster sugar
grated rind and juice of
   1 small orange
2 cm/1 inch piece fresh
   root ginger, peeled
   and chopped
4 firm pears, such as
   Williams or
   Conference
175 g/6 oz plain dark
   chocolate
150 ml/¼ pint double
   cream
25 g/1 oz golden
   granulated sugar

1 Pour the red wine with 150 ml/¼ pint of water into a heavy-based saucepan and stir in the sugar, the orange rind and juice with the ginger. Place over a gentle heat and bring slowly to the boil, stirring occasionally until the sugar has dissolved. Once the sugar has dissolved, boil steadily for 5 minutes, then remove from the heat.

2 Using a potato peeler, carefully peel the pears, leaving the stalks intact. If preferred, gently remove the cores from the base of each pear. (You can, if you prefer, leave the cores intact for a neater finish.) If necessary, cut a very thin slice off the base of each pear so they sit upright.

3 Carefully stand the pears in the hot syrup, return to the heat, cover with a lid and simmer gently for 20 minutes or until tender, turning the pears occasionally. Remove from the heat and leave to cool in the syrup, turning occasionally. Using a slotted spoon, transfer the pears to a large dish.

4 Strain the syrup, then bring back to the boil and boil rapidly until reduced and syrupy. Add the chocolate, cream and sugar to the saucepan and bring very slowly to the boil, stirring constantly until the chocolate has melted. Arrange the pears on serving plates and carefully spoon over the chocolate sauce. Serve immediately.

Raspberry & Hazelnut Meringue Cake

Ingredients
Cuts into 8 slices

For the meringue

4 large egg whites
¼ tsp cream of tartar
225 g/8 oz caster sugar
75 g/3 oz hazelnuts,
   skinned, toasted and
   finely ground

For the filling

300 ml/½ pint double
   cream
1 tbsp icing sugar
1–2 tbsp raspberry-
   flavoured liqueur
   (optional)
350 g/12 oz fresh
   raspberries

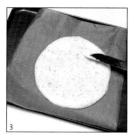

1 Preheat the oven to 140°C/ 275°F/Gas Mark 1. Line 2 baking sheets with non-stick baking paper and draw a 20.5 cm/8 inch circle on each. Whisk the egg whites and cream of tartar until soft peaks form then gradually beat in the sugar, 2 tablespoons at a time.

2 Beat well after each addition until the whites are stiff and glossy. Using a metal spoon or rubber spatula, gently fold in the ground hazelnuts.

3 Divide the mixture evenly between the two circles and spread neatly. Swirl one of the circles to make a decorative top layer. Bake in the preheated oven for about 1½ hours, until crisp and dry. Turn off the oven and allow the meringues to cool for 1 hour. Transfer to a wire rack to cool completely. Carefully peel off the papers.

4 For the filling, whip the cream, icing sugar and liqueur, if using, together until soft peaks form. Place the flat round on a serving plate. Spread over most of the cream, reserving some for decorating and arrange the raspberries in concentric circles over the cream.

5 Place the swirly meringue on top of the cream and raspberries, pressing down gently. Pipe the remaining cream on to the meringue, decorate with a few raspberries and serve.

Spicy White Chocolate Mousse

Ingredients
Serves 4–6

6 cardamom pods
125 ml/4 fl oz milk
3 bay leaves
200 g/7 oz white
   chocolate
300 ml/½ pint double
   cream
3 medium egg whites
1–2 tsp cocoa powder,
   sifted, for dusting

1 Tap the cardamom pods lightly so they split. Remove the seeds, then, using a pestle and mortar, crush lightly. Pour the milk into a small saucepan and add the crushed seeds and the bay leaves. Bring to the boil gently over a medium heat. Remove from the heat, cover and leave in a warm place for at least 30 minutes to infuse.

2 Break the chocolate into small pieces and place in a heatproof bowl set over a saucepan of gently simmering water. Ensure the water is not touching the base of the bowl. When the chocolate has melted remove the bowl from the heat and stir until smooth.

3 Whip the cream until it has slightly thickened and holds its shape, but does not form peaks. Reserve. Whisk the egg whites in a clean, grease-free bowl until stiff and standing in soft peaks.

4 Strain the milk through a sieve into the cooled, melted chocolate and beat until smooth. Spoon the chocolate mixture into the egg whites, then using a large metal spoon, fold gently. Add the whipped cream and fold in gently.

5 Spoon into a large serving dish or individual small cups. Chill in the refrigerator for 3–4 hours. Just before serving, dust with a little sifted cocoa powder and then serve.

Strawberry Flan

Ingredients
Serves 6

Sweet pastry
175 g/6 oz plain flour
50 g/2 oz butter
50 g/2 oz white
  vegetable fat
2 tsp caster sugar
1 medium egg yolk,
  beaten

For the filling
1 medium egg, plus 1
  extra egg yolk
50 g/2 oz caster sugar
25 g/1 oz plain flour
300 ml/½ pint milk
few drops of vanilla
  essence
450 g/1 lb strawberries,
  cleaned and hulled
mint leaves, to
  decorate

1 Preheat the oven to 200˚C/ 400˚F/Gas Mark 6. Place the flour, butter and vegetable fat in a food processor and blend until the mixture resembles fine breadcrumbs. Stir in the sugar, then with the machine running, add the egg yolk and enough water to make a fairly stiff dough. Knead lightly, cover and chill in the refrigerator for 30 minutes.

2 Roll out the pastry and use to line a 23 cm/9 inch loose - bottomed flan tin. Place a piece of greaseproof paper in the pastry case and cover with baking beans or rice. Bake in the preheated oven for 15–20 minutes, until just firm. Reserve until cool.

3 Make the filling by whisking the eggs and sugar together until thick and pale. Gradually stir in the flour and then the milk. Pour into a small saucepan and simmer for 3–4 minutes stirring throughout.

4 Add the vanilla essence to taste, then pour into a bowl and leave to cool. Cover with greaseproof paper to prevent a skin from forming.

5 When the filling is cold, whisk until smooth then pour on to the cooked flan case. Slice the strawberries and arrange on the top of the filling. Decorate with the mint leaves and serve.

CHEF'S TIP
In the summer, when the choice of fruit is greater why not try topping the flan with a variety of mixed fruits. Arrange strawberries, raspberries, kiwi fruit and blueberries on top of the filling.

Topsy Turvy Pudding

Ingredients
Serves 6

For the topping
175 g/6 oz demerara
   sugar
2 oranges

For the sponge
175 g/6 oz butter,
   softened
175 g/6 oz caster sugar
3 medium eggs, beaten
175 g/6 oz self-raising
   flour, sifted
50 g/2 oz plain dark
   chocolate, melted
grated rind of 1 orange
25 g/1 oz cocoa powder,
   sifted
custard or soured
   cream, to serve

1 Preheat the oven to 180°C/ 350°F/Gas Mark 4, 10 minutes before baking. Lightly oil a 20.5 cm/8 inch deep round loose-based cake tin. Place the demerara sugar and 3 tablespoons of water in a small heavy-based saucepan and heat gently until the sugar has dissolved. Swirl the saucepan or stir with a clean wooden spoon to ensure the sugar has dissolved, then bring to the boil and boil rapidly until a golden caramel is formed. Pour into the base of the tin and leave to cool.

2 For the sponge, cream the butter and sugar together until light and fluffy. Gradually beat in the eggs a little at a time, beating well between each addition. Add a spoonful of flour after each addition to prevent the mixture curdling. Add the melted chocolate and then stir well. Fold in the orange rind, self-raising flour and sifted cocoa powder and mix well.

3 Remove the peel from both oranges taking care to remove as much of the pith as possible. Thinly slice the peel into strips and then slice the oranges. Arrange the peel and then the orange slices over the caramel. Top with the sponge mixture and level the top.

4 Place the tin on a baking sheet and bake in the preheated oven for 40–45 minutes or until well risen, golden brown and an inserted skewer comes out clean. Remove from the oven, leave for about 5 minutes, invert onto a serving plate and sprinkle with cocoa powder. Serve with either custard or soured cream.

White Chocolate Cheesecake

Ingredients
Cuts into 16 slices

For the base

150 g/5 oz digestive biscuits, finely crumbed
50 g/2 oz whole almonds, lightly toasted and finely crumbed
50 g/2 oz butter, melted
½ tsp almond essence

For the filling

350 g/12 oz good-quality white chocolate, chopped
125 ml /4 fl oz double cream
700 g/1½ lb cream cheese, softened
50 g/2 oz caster sugar
4 large eggs
2 tbsp Amaretto or almond-flavour liqueur

For the topping

450 ml/¾ pint soured cream
50 g/2 oz caster sugar
½ tsp almond or vanilla essence
white chocolate curls, to decorate

1 Preheat the oven to 180°C/ 350°F/Gas Mark 4. Lightly oil a 23 x 7.5 cm /9 x 3 inch springform tin. Mix the melted butter and almond essence, with the biscuit and almond crumbs. Pour the mixture into the tin and press on to the bottom and up the sides to within 1 cm/½ inch of the top. Bake in the preheated oven for 5 minutes to set. Remove and transfer to a wire rack. Reduce the oven temperature to 150°C/ 300°F/Gas Mark 2.

2 Heat the white chocolate and cream in a saucepan over a low heat, stirring constantly until melted. Remove and cool. Beat the cream cheese and sugar until smooth. Add the eggs, one at a time, beating well after each addition. Slowly beat in the cooled white chocolate cream and the Amaretto and pour into the baked crust.

3 Place on a baking tray and bake for 45–55 minutes, until the edge of the cake is firm, but the centre is slightly soft. Reduce the oven temperature if the top begins to brown. Remove to a wire rack, and increase the oven temperature to 200°C/400°F/Gas Mark 6.

4 To make the topping, beat the soured cream, sugar and almond or vanilla essence until smooth and gently pour over the cheesecake. Return to the oven and bake for another 5 minutes to set. Turn off the oven and leave the cheesecake to cool, with the oven door open, for one hour.

5 Transfer to a wire rack and run a sharp knife around the edge of the crust to separate from the tin. Chill in the refrigerator. Remove from the tin, decorate with white chocolate curls and serve.

White Chocolate Terrine with Red Fruit Compote

Ingredients
Serves 8

225 g/8 oz white chocolate

300 ml/½ pint double cream

225 g/8 oz full fat soft cream cheese

2 tbsp finely grated orange rind

125 g/4 oz caster sugar

350 g/12 oz mixed summer fruits, such as strawberries, blueberries and raspberries

1 tbsp Cointreau

sprigs of fresh mint, to decorate

1 Set the freezer to rapid freeze at least 2 hours before required. Lightly oil and line a 450 g/1 lb loaf tin with clingfilm, taking care to keep the clingfilm as wrinkle free as possible. Break the white chocolate into small pieces and place in a heatproof bowl set over a saucepan of gently simmering water. Leave for 20 minutes or until melted, then remove from the heat and stir until smooth. Leave to cool.

2 Whip the cream until soft peaks form. Beat the cream cheese until soft and creamy, then beat in the grated orange rind and 50 g/2 oz of the caster sugar. Mix well, then fold in the whipped cream and then the cooled melted white chocolate.

3 Spoon the mixture into the prepared loaf tin and level the surface. Place in the freezer and freeze for at least 4 hours or until frozen. Once frozen, remember to return the freezer to its normal setting.

4 Place the fruits with the remaining sugar in a heavy-based saucepan and heat gently, stirring occasionally, until the sugar has dissolved and the juices from the fruits are just beginning to run. Add the Cointreau.

5 Dip the loaf tin into hot water for 30 seconds and invert onto a serving plate. Carefully remove the tin and clingfilm. Decorate with sprigs of mint and serve sliced with the prepared red fruit compote.

This is a Star Fire book
First Published in 2003

02 04 05 03 01

1 3 5 7 9 10 8 6 4 2

Star Fire is part of The Foundry Creative Media Company Limited
Crabtree Hall, Crabtree Lane, Fulham, London, SW6 6TY
Visit the Foundry website: www.foundry.co.uk

visit our cookery website: www.practicalrecipes.com

ISBN: 1-903817-88-9

The CIP record for this book is available from the British Library

Printed in Croatia

Acknowledgements

Authors: Catherine Atkinson, Juliet Barker, Liz Martin,
Gina Steer, Carol Tennant, Mari Mereid Williams,
Elizabeth Wolf-Cohen, Simone Wright

Editorial Consultant: Gina Steer

Editors: Michelle Clare, Karen Fitzpatrick, Vicky Garrard, Julia Rolf
Photography: Colin Bowling and Paul Forrester

Home Economists and Stylists: Jacqueline Bellefontaine,
Mandy Phipps, Vicki Smallwood and Penny Stephens

Design Team: Helen Courtney, Jennifer Bishop,
Lucy Bradbury and Chris Herbert

All props supplied by Barbara Stewart at Surfaces

Note

Recipes using uncooked eggs should be avoided by infants, the
elderly, pregnant women and anyone suffering from an illness.